YOUGHAL'S FADING FOOTSTEPS

The Humour,
History
& People
of East Cork
& West Waterford.

MIKE HACKETT

GW00713273

LOCAL HISTORY COLLECTION

ON STREAM

Published 1994
by
On Stream Publications
Ltd. Cloghroe, Blarney,
Co. Cork. Ireland. Tel/Fax
021 385798

ISBN: 1 897685 95 5

Front Cover - Clockgate

Back Cover – Cecil Pratt was a shopkeeper, angler and angling correspondent. Just a month before his death, he caught a specimen plaice of 7lbs. $2^1/_2$ozs for which he received a special award.
He composed his own epitaph with the help of his two friends, Christy Browne and Frank Cooper.

Acknowledgements

To my wife, Mary, for her advice, tolerance and typing.

This is a Youghal Credit Union Community Project

The author gratefully acknowledges the assistance of the following in the production and launching of this book:

Colm Keane
The Devonshire Arms Hotel

Pa Aherne
Gerardine Brown
Eileen Burns
John Casey
Liam Burke
Bridget Carey
Billy Collins
Phil Cullinane
Kay Donnelly
Sean Fitzgerald
Betty Fitzgibbon
Bridie Forrest

John Griffin
Mary Hackett Snr.
Sheila Keogh
Pauline McCarthy
Nora McGrath
Billy Matthis
Maureen Morris
Clare O'Brien
Fr. Anthony O'Brien
Mick O'Brien
John O'Brien
Kitty O'Connor

Angela O'Connor
Sean O'Keeffe
Peg O'Shea
Maureen O'Sullivan
Simon Pomphrett
Field Printers
Micky Roche
Tony Simkins
Billy Swayne
Paddy Swayne
Molly Veale
Jimmy Whyte

CONTENTS

INTRODUCTION

"You are the sixth Michael Hackett in successive generations that I have known," said an old woman to me one day when I played as a child in Brown Street. It was about 1954 and Mrs. Ellen O'Brien who was eighty years old was recalling her youth in Knockanore. My ancestors had lived in her locality and she went on to tell that when she was about ten years of age, she would listen to my great-great-great-grandfather telling stories as an old man by the fireside. The period spoken of, when she was ten, must have been 1884 and the old man at ninety made a link in memory back to the late 1700s.

Now I often regret that I hadn't more sense to listen to the stories that she in turn related from several generations before her. How fascinating that an old man talking to a child, who subsequently in her own old age spoke to another child, could result in the social history of two hundred years being recorded. Fortunately as a post office official for the last thirty years I have met many more people who have given me their treasured stories to pass on, and which I now relate to you to enjoy.

All who read this book will have their own Michael Hacketts and also their Mrs. O'Briens, by other names, and so to all those, we dedicate this social history in our area.

Mike Hackett

FROM WHENCE WE HAVE COME
A brief history of Youghal

Despite whatever tribal feuds were going on, Ireland was a peaceful enough island in early historical times. You have the earthen *liosanna* on hilltops around the countryside as examples of early fortifications. Apart from any disagreement with the neighbours, the protection was needed to keep out the wolves and wild boars who roamed the woodland freely.

In the 6th century, there were three monastic centres in close proximity with St. Declan at Ardmore (416 a.d.), St. Molanfide at Molana Abbey (501 a.d.) and St. Coran at Summerfield (575 a.d.)

Ardmore proudly guards St. Declan's Well and grave as its heritage. Molana Island, four miles up river and accessible by a causeway, has extensive remains of the monastery of St. Molanfide, while at Summerfield, south of the town, there is St. Coran's Well. All testify to the early Christianity in this area.

The large sheltered harbour of Youghal, with the great river Blackwater beckoning, must have been very attractive to the Norse invaders of the ninth century. The Danes landed to establish a base at Eochaill (the wood of the Yews) and from that early time the town has seen a remarkable variety of history.

Later, in the twelfth century, came the Normans and as was

said, 'they became more Irish than the Irish themselves.' St. Mary's Church was built during this period and part of that original structure still exists, incorporated in the present building.

The town grew successfully to become a fine Norman stronghold and in 1202 was granted its first Royal Charter. Other relics of the Norman influence can be seen at the Dominican ruins of North Abbey, Knights Templars of Rhincrew site and in the lower parts of the town walls. Dominican monks at North Abbey, the Franciscans at South Abbey and the Benedictines at North Main Street must have given a great religious aura to the town in the years before the Reformation.

As well, in 1464, the College of Our Lady of Youghal adjoining St. Mary's Church was founded to educate seminarians. It was called by that name because of the small ivory statue found in a piece of timber on the mud-flats north of Youghal. The statue of Our Lady of Youghal is now on display in the Dominican Church, Pope's Quay, Cork.

Ireland became known abroad as the island of saints and scholars and Youghal, with its monasteries and college, was playing its part.

This was all to change because, following the Gerardine Wars, came the Reformation with the closing of all religious establishments. The Plantation of Munster gave Walter Raleigh 42,000 acres, including the towns of Lismore, Tallow and Youghal. He was Mayor of the town during 1588 -'89.

Tobacco is first said to have been smoked by Walter Raleigh, at Myrtle Grove, near St. Mary's Collegiate Church and the first potatoes in this part of the world were grown there also.

A local folklore story tells of a servant throwing a bucket of water over Walter Raleigh as he relaxed under a great yew tree with smoke pouring from his mouth. That same servant was asked to prepare the potatoes from the garden for dinner and, not having seen the likes before, ended up cooking the stalks of the plant.

A great period in shipping made Youghal one of the busiest ports in Ireland, exporting wool, iron, timber, fish, cattle and linen. As early as 1678, thirty-three ships were registered in the local port. By comparison, Cork then had twenty-four registered ships and Kinsale had twenty-two.

Through all this, the native Irish were both outside and inside the walls. Country dwellers were native Irish speakers bringing their Gaelic ways to town on market days, but at night all natives without permits had to be outside the walls.

In Youghal, the area south of the clock Gate was enclosed to a lesser extent and was the 'Irishtown' of the community. Cork Hill on the north side and Windmill Hill on the south, being outside the town walls, were unprotected 'Irishtown' locations.

When the Reformation period had passed, a new Parish Church was built near the old Quaker graveyard at Ashe Street in 1796. This had its steeple removed for safety reasons earlier this century, but otherwise it has lasted well and of course will celebrate its bi-centennial in 1996.

The arrival of the Presentation Order of nuns in 1834 signalled a new era in education for the ordinary (poor) of the town. A school, convent and chapel were subsequently built to cater for the large population. Then, in 1857, the Christian Brothers came to teach boys in a big house on Strand Street owned by the Duke of Devonshire. This building served until the 1960s when two new boys' schools were built, primary and secondary.

Loreto nuns came to town in 1862 at North Main Street, then moved to Strand House before settling at Lighthouse Hill. Ashton Court, the splendid home of Samuel J. Merrick, was later acquired for expansion and this now forms the main portion of the modern secondary school. Members of the Presentation Order, Loreto Order and the Christian Brothers still teach in town.

Since the Normans first marked the foundations of the town walls, Youghal was a garrison town and so there was always an army presence of some kind. In later centuries, soldiers from England, Scotland and Wales were based here. Many of those stayed, and in the process became integrated into the fabric of society by marrying local girls.

Two hundred and sixty years after Walter Raleigh, the potato had become the staple diet of the eight million Irish population. When the blight struck the crop in 1847, millions died from hunger, and many more emigrated on the coffin ships. After that terrible famine era, the population of the country had dropped by over two million. It was to reduce further to four million by 1911 through continuing emigration.

Youghal was not the worst hit, being a garrison town and because the grain, so badly needed, was housed in the corn stores, awaiting the ships. Not so lucky was the population of the surrounding countryside as they flocked to the town for help. The sad evidence can be seen at the famine graveyards in Grange and Ballymacoda. For those who reached town, it is said that the 'help' tickets were given out from a shop at the top of Brown Street, and from there the poor misfortunate people went to the quayside stores where the soup, plus doss (hay bag) were supplied. For years after, in a plot behind the stores, the mounds of the shallow graves could be traced in the grass. It was the resting place of the hungry for whom the help had been too late.

1861 saw the train bringing holiday-makers to the five-mile long strand, away from the hot inland towns in summer. Some got off, stayed here and settled down.

The twentieth century started off with on-going heavy emigration, before others, in large numbers, went to fight in the First World War. Then, following the establishment of the Free State, Irish soldiers came to occupy the military barracks at Cork Hill. This resulted in men from all over the country forming friendships to marry local girls.

Seafield Fabrics, Blackwater Cottons and Youghal Carpets brought the industrial boom of the 1950s and 60s. The first and second brought people from the North of England, who were experienced in textile manufacturing and they settled with us. Youghal Carpets also attracted workers from East Cork and more so from West Waterford to join our community and share our lifestyle.

You will agree that our Town has had a chequered background unequalled by most, but despite all that, minorities can be found who retained their pure culture.

Those traditionalists can speak a language, can dance and sing like their forefathers did hundreds of years ago. Thankfully, such ways have endured but generally human behaviour tends to blend in familiarity. How much it occurred in Youghal, through all that history, is a large conjecture.

Dominican Ruins, North Abbey

FATHER O'NEILL

Cork City has its Fr. Matthew watching over it in Patrick Street through all climates and moods. Likewise, Youghal has its priestly statue of Fr. O'Neill, who stands tall at the '98 Memorial Park, or as the locals call it, Green Park.

For years there was one great difference between them, in that the Youghal man had only one hand. It was broken off during the Troubles around 1920, and for seventy two years the priest stood there, uncomplaining. Then, in 1992, Con McCarthy, a local man, at the behest of the U.D.C. sculpted a new hand from marble for Father O'Neill to coincide with the remodelling of the Park.

People often ask about Fr. O'Neill and the background to the memorial. Peter O'Neill was born in Conna in 1747 and got his early education at a hedge school near Inch. He went to college in Paris, was ordained, and returned to Ireland in 1781. Skibbereen was his first post as Curate before moving to Ballymacoda as Parish Priest in 1786. In this period land rents soared, causing the United Irishmen movement to spread to Imokilly. The exorbitantly high tithes demanded of the people caused the unrest which led to the 1798 rising in Wexford.

At that time, a man called Patrick Murphy of Ballymacoda was murdered. It had been feared that he was about to inform on some of the local United Irishmen. Fr. O'Neill was the priest for the area and was arrested on suspicion of having knowledge of the deed, although pleading innocent. He was brought to Youghal and without trial was given a flogging. Halfway up the jail steps, where it crosses with Ashe Street, was a ball alley and here Fr. O'Neill received 249 lashes. During the next few days, he was threatened with death constantly in an effort to get information. After imprisonment in Geneva Barracks at Waterford, he was transported to Australia as a convict.

Consternation over the whole affair continued here at home and resulted in Fr. O'Neill returning to Ireland in 1803. Bishop Coppinger of Cloyne then re-appointed him as Parish Priest of Ballymacoda, where he went on to build churches and schools.

On 29th July, 1835, Fr. O'Neill died and is buried in Ballymacoda Churchyard, but his memory lives on as the local G.A.A. team are called 'Fr. O'Neills.'

GREAT GAS

Children huddle at Mill Road Cross in the cool twilight of the evening as they await the arrival of their idol. Not for them the stars of pop or film. Just an ordinary local man who means heaven to these children. A shout of joy goes up. Here he comes - the local lamplighter!

Up goes the ladder against the lamp-post and he climbs up to turn on the gas and light the mantles. Twenty small faces, with mouths open, watch his every move. An eerie light shines down before he makes a small adjustment to brighten it a bit. The crossroad is lit up and the fun starts. Dancing, chasing and games, out to the curve of the darkness, as playful shrieks and laughter fill the night air.

Incidentally, in the earlier part of this century, the Urban District Council of Youghal thought that the full moon was sufficient to light the town for three nights every month. This meant that the public gaslights were not lit and the lamplighter got those three nights off.

People often refer to some character as a 'Gas Man,' meaning a funny entertainer. Apart from the 'windbag' theory, perhaps this originated with the lamplighter or Gasman as he went joyfully on his rounds, lighting up the darkness for the kids of the different areas. Sometimes he would be met a good way off and escorted gleefully to the lamp. It was a ripe situation for story-telling, especially ghost stories, and most lamplighters were good at it.

The Youghal Gas House was located between Tallow Street and Mill Road at the North side of town and it was built in 1830, as the figures on the front of the big slate-roofed building boldly said. Dotted around it, like monster canisters, were the huge gasometers (storage tanks) which could grow upwards as the pressure of gas increased inside them. To small kids, a glance in the gateway was to see a vision of science fiction. We often wondered when the red coke-cinders would get near the tanks to blow half of the town up. Hopefully it would be on the morning of some school day, but even our wishful elastic imaginations could not visualise it blowing up the school building which was over a mile away.

Within the big hall was the furnace house with its steel-plated flooring, the process of taking gas and tar from coal was done. At ground level, you had the great furnaces, burning coke (until the 1950s when they were changed to oil), and above them in a row you had the retorts where the coal was roasted in airless chambers. Pipes then brought the gas and tar from the retorts to their respective containers.

As the gas left the retorts, its pipes went along a water trough to cool it. It was then washed through more water to clean it and, lastly, passed through oxide clay to purify it.

Children in town with whooping cough were brought by their mothers to these purifying oxide clay beds and allowed to play around them. Apparently, after a couple of hours breathing the mixed vapours of that atmosphere, the whooping cough symptoms waned and the child would go home much improved.

The tar made its way to an underground tank from which it would be hand-pumped out for sale. Occasionally the tar pipe would get blocked and would have to be cleared with an auger. This was a long steel rod with a large corkscrew head to free the solidified tar and at times the screw would have to be reddened in the furnace first. The uses for tar were many and varied from tarring boat-bottoms for fishermen to protecting tin roofs from the weather. In earlier years, all houses were whitewashed except for a two-foot section near the ground which was tarred to hide the mud splashes from the dirt tracks. Then later came the tarring of the roads.

When working at the Gas Works, everybody wore boots without laces. The reason for this was that now and then small red cinders would fly out of the retort and if one went down inside the boot, there would be no time to open laces

Another occupational hazard was the spattering tar. Speaking recently to a retired stoker, he told of getting spot burns on his arms and hands many times. Those burn marks are still to be clearly seen after forty years.

Before we leave the furnace (retort) house, just let me tell about how the stokers would sometimes allow curious children in to see the fires and would say, "You be good, that is what hell is like!" Children who lived in the area of the Gas House were always well-behaved.

In the home of a local character, on a winter's night, I watched as he prepared, by gaslight, for a date. Marbles, or glassyalleys as we called them, were the rage at the time and we all treasured whatever few we possessed. While washing his face, the character presented me with a lovely big white marble. I was delighted as I examined it in the glow of the gaslight. However, on turning it around in my hand, I discovered a perfect eye on the other side. It was his glass eye that was in my hand. He grabbed it before I dropped it with fright.

An old story tells about a publican opening at 7 a.m., which was a special exemption on a fair day morning. The first two customers through the door had nothing to do with the fair. They were two workers from the Gas House, who had been working all night. "Two pints, please!" Paddy the publican had just tapped a new barrel of porter in readiness for the busy day ahead. Up on the counter went the first two pints to the thirsty blackened men. Then, "Uggh!" and another "Uggh!" - the porter was 'casky', slightly burnt and not fit to be sold. The publican was very disappointed as he replaced the barrel but the two lads consoled him by offering to drink the 'casky' porter for free. "The brewery rep. will allow you for it," they assured him.

A few days later, the brewery rep. arrived to hear of the 'casky' porter and asked to see the barrel. When he discovered that it was empty, he regretted that he could not give compensation and Paddy the publican had to pay for the porter.

Of all the personnel involved in the operation of the Gas Works, the hardest job was surely that of the stoker. He worked in the furnace house, feeding coal in through the great cylindrical doors. The heat was such that, even in winter, the stokers were stripped to the waist and of course covered in coal dust. A story from the local G.A.A. history book tells of such a man going straight from work on a summer's evening to play a match with the local team. When he appeared out on the pitch, the opposition intended to object, thinking that he was a sailor from a coal boat. They laughed when the truth of the black man was pointed out to them. (The book called 'Up the Youghal Boys' is by Frank Keane).

The Gas Works meant a lot to the local community. Gas was used for cooking and lighting in homes and for public lighting on the streets. The by-product called coke was sold for about half the price of coal and was great to heat ranges and stoves. A lot of employment and services depended on the Gas House. There were sailors, dockers, horse and cart owners, delivery men, office workers, service men, stokers and the lamplighters.

A common sight in those years was to see the horse and carts trundling slowly from the quayside, loaded with coal, up through the main street, on their way to the Gas House. It was a special type of coal and was in big lump form as it passed by on the high-sided carts. A sad feature was that when a cart-wheel would hit a pot-hole, a few of those lumps would fall off and be quickly picked up by local people. At every corner on the journey, you would see some poor old woman, draped in a big black woollen shawl, waiting for the lumps to fall off. She would then discreetly venture on to the road and place the coal in the basket under her shawl. After a couple of hours, the woman would have a basketful of coal, weighing about a quarter of a hundredweight, to light her fire for a day or two, and home she would quietly go. The men's part of this prevent-waste campaign was at the quayside. Having unloaded its cargo, the vessel would sail with the dropping tide to reveal a heavy deposit of coal along the bottom of the quay wall. This would have fallen between the boat and the quay during the few days of unloading. As soon as the tide dropped low enough, the men would climb down the quayside ladders and wade into the water to retrieve what would amount to several bags of coal.

Speaking of the quays, the vessels mainly used were the Kathleen and May, the De Wadden, and the ill-fated Nellie Fleming. The Nellie foundered with the loss of all five sailors between Milford Haven and Youghal in 1936 during a storm.

Locally manufactured coal-gas fuelled homes in towns and cities for about a hundred and fifty years. Youghal was one of those and almost every house had piped gas. By way of payment, the gas meter was well known, located where the pipe entered the house and it swallowed the big one-penny pieces. Every month the meter man came to clear it of the coins and there was great speculation as hundreds of them were counted on the kitchen table. Whatever was over and above the meter reading was returned to the woman of the house as a bonus. It was time to buy the cream crackers and Marietta biscuits - a great treat.

The large lump coal, less the gas and tar, was called coke and was sold to the locals every morning. Customers paid for it at an office window just inside the gate, and in return, they got a brass ticket to hand to the weighman. A triangular ticket was for a hundredweight and a round one for a half. As the queue waited patiently, clutching their brass pieces, from inside the furnace house would come a man, stripped to the waist, covered in black, rolling a huge steel barrow of hot coals. This was doused with buckets of water and as the steam cloud rose skywards, the red slowly turned to grey to reveal the huge cinders. It still had a lot of burning left in it and was great to keep a fire red.

Coke was only half the weight of the original coal, and a big sackful was just a half hundredweight. To see a cart with ten bags of coke piled high was firstly to wonder at the strength of the horse pulling it. Then on closer inspection, noticing the larger bulges of coke, onlookers understood. A pensioner told of how red and hot the coke got when burning in her range-cooker. So hot, she said, that it burned out the steel quicker than coal would have, and she had to get a new range installed. It was a God-send for poor families being such good value, and every little backyard in town would have a corner for it.

During the early 1940s, while the Second World War was on, all coal was very scarce and most houses were using just timber and turf for their open fires. It was very hard to get goods into Ireland because of the submarine menace and only necessary requirements were imported. Included was the Gasworks' coal to keep the cities and towns as near to normal as possible.

In this dangerous period for shipping, the coal boats made the shortest crossing of the Irish Sea to the Republic. It meant coming into Dublin and so the coal was transported by rail to the Gas Works in distant parts of the country. Because of the risk, the trouble and the cost, only the minimum amount of fuel was received and of course resulted in less gas and coke being available. A shortage of gas could somehow be tolerated because of the lights curfew after dark when all the lamps had to be out or the windows blackened. The shortage of coke, on the other hand, was greatly felt because normal domestic coal was unavailable and most of the turf was wet. Tough years they were.

Opening time for the sale of coke was at 9 a.m. and during the Emergency of the Second World War, a long queue would form well before that. Some people were credited with standing at the gate from 3 a.m. to be sure of getting the one bag, which was all that was given per customer.

Many hardships were endured during those long hours, along that white-washed roadside wall of the Gas Works. Old and young queued side by side in the cold of the winter mornings clutching their brass ticket, which had been purchased the previous evening in readiness. There are many versions about the way people passed those waiting hours. Mostly they just chatted but an odd person would sing quietly or pray the rosary. A few would have the luxury of clutching a wrapped heated brick to their chest, while others would rely on extra clothes for warmth.

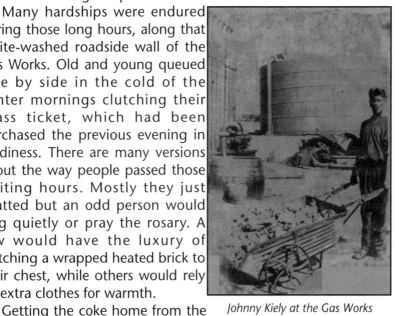

Johnny Kiely at the Gas Works

Getting the coke home from the Gas House was difficult before motor transport. Some people were lucky to have a homemade timber barrow, and those who had a bicycle could jam the bag in the frame and push it. Yet some others brought it home on their backs and for those who had the spare few bob, you had the pony and cart owners to bring it to the door.

The arrival of electrical current foretold the end of the Gas Works era. Nothing could compare with it in its day, but that day was now gone. The closure of the local Gas Works in 1963 brought to an end a part of history which had been a gigantic step on mankind's road to better living conditions.

THE TRAIN TO YOUGHAL

Oh! for the seabreeze, far away from the hot city on a summer's day!

The train to Youghal was a cheap escape for many families in Cork City to a haven of open space with fresh air, the seaside and lots of fun. As many as twenty trains would leave Glanmire Road station on any Sunday in July and August, filled with people of all ages. It always amused me to think that the trains all arrived at the seaside full, while the first few to return back to Cork in the evening would only half-full. The answer was simple enough - the last few trains would be chock-a-block with passengers.

On arrival at Youghal station the train was longer than any of the three platforms, but that was no problem for the sea-seekers. Some jumped just as quickly on to the tracks as others did where the carriages had a platform. Everybody, laden down, rushed out the railway gate and over towards the sea wall for a first glimpse of the broad Atlantic Ocean and five miles of golden beach stretching away as far as can be seen in the shimmering sunlight.

'Is the tide in or out?', 'Is there a breeze?' 'Stay with me,' 'Mind the go-car,' 'Catch my hand,' and 'Don't drag the bag along the ground', were the cries. Everybody carried luggage of some kind - bags of food, the kettle, teapot, buckets and spades, towels and togs, sportsgear, go-cars, rugs and even raincoats. To the young it was a tremendous adventure, to others a romantic break and to the not-so-young, it was the renewing of fond memories.

Out along the promenade they poured, each group looking for the type of place to suit them. Flat sand for games, wet sand for castles, further up for a nice place to picnic and up in the dunes for shelter from the breeze and privacy. Change the clothes and hit the water fast, those lovely waves created by some invisible force racing to the shore, never-endingly. After the dip, time to eat. Someone is sent with the kettle to buy sixpence worth of boiling water at a nearby shack to make the tea. Afterwards the children venture to ride one of the small ponies along the beach for a few pence. Then the games - all kinds of pitches and goal-posts drawn on the sand. People falling everywhere without hurt. A dream come true.

Adults would go to Clancy's for a pint of porter while the kids got a few bob for Perks' Funfair. There was a lovely relaxing holiday mood about Clancy's Railway bar; everybody in good form. Wives, who would not dare be seen in a pub at home, now side by side at the counter with their husbands, not to mention the baby in the pram outside drinking porter instead of milk.

Many locals availed of the visiting throngs to make a few bob. The bathing boxes were the domain of the old women with the huge black shawls. It was sixpence per hour for the use of a box and it guaranteed absolute privacy in an age when the body was well covered at all times. There is a story told about a man being asked by an old woman to use her bathing box and he politely replied that he could not because he suffered from claustrophobia. 'Ah sure don't worry,' said she, 'jump in the box, we'll let the door open and I'll shade you with my big black shawl.'

A long row of barrows held edibles like kelp seaweed, carrigeen moss and periwinkles. Sold in bags for a few pence, following the pints in Clancy's, they would all taste delicious. A pin was given with the periwinkles to help extract them from the shells and anybody complaining about the price would be told, 'Sure the pin is free.'

Small shops along the prom sold things like beach balls, postcards, buckets and spades, wind-blowers and ice-cream.

Over at the Showboat Ballroom, the late great Mick Delahunty and his orchestra were getting ready for an evening of ballroom dancing and he was a good man to play in the Glen Miller style. At the nearby Strand Palace the early dance was already in full swing with a second session beginning at 9 o'clock.

Claycastle, with its lovely grass covering, was the location for the open-air theatre. A family of show people would assemble a timber platform to be used as a stage and place about twenty chairs in small rows in front of it. A light rope connected stakes around the perimeter and this encouraged the audience to contribute before sitting down to enjoy the show. A threepenny bit was expected for a seat while it was free to stand and watch from outside. The cap would be passed around now and then to those standing.

Singing, dancing, jokes and magic tricks made up the show and a new performance would start every hour. Older people who had given up swimming, tennis and such active pursuits, would sit all evening watching as many as five consecutive shows and, of course, paying five threepenny bits. It was such a remarkable, accomplished theatrical family, that in all those hours, no song, joke or trick was repeated.

Time to gather all the gear, make the short journey wearily but happily to the train and hopefully find a seat. All are tired but renewed and full of the joys of life. The steam engine has been turned on the huge turntable and has moved up to the other end of the train, faced for home. As it slowly chugs away into the twilight, the waves can still be faintly heard breaking on the shore, as if in a fond farewell from the seaside.

Coming off the turntable at Youghal
Photo courtesy Colm Creedon, Railway Historian

YOUGHAL'S COLOURFUL CHARACTERS

Fine Buildings, streets filled with history and spacious parks are the framework for a happy successful town, but it takes people to bring it alive. Somebody said that people are the lifeblood of a town, and characters are the measure of the spirit of the people.

Most people nowadays have plentiful food, clothes and warmth, but go back to the earlier part of this century to find a much different situation. The 'troubles' were going on, hunger and poverty were widespread and T.B. was rampant. Yet there were characters who could make the people laugh in spite of all and no words of mine could pay proper tribute to them.

Before the coming of radio and T.V., daytime amusement could be had by meeting the many characters who were part of our town. Then, as if the locals were not enough, Youghal had morethan its share of mirth with much diversified activities. One had only to think of the visiting tars (sailors), soldiers, fishermen and holiday-makers, who mixed with the locals to create a vibrant society.

A great entertainer, in the Irish or English language, was the late **John Fitzgerald.** In bygone days, he had a piece of land at Greencloyne, adjoining Mrs. Hannon's house and garden. She kept hens with chickens and would put them over into John's field for a bit of a run. If the chickens were very small, she would put over a saucer of milk & bread as well.

John arrived out at his field one day to find it alive with Mrs. Hannon's hens and chickens. Now he didn't mind much but he felt that she should have asked him. He noticed her as she put out her washing on the line and he gave her a shout: "What are those hens doing on my land?"

"Oh John, they must have flown over," she answered.

"What about the chickens?"

"Oh John, they must have flown over also."

"Tell me, Mrs. Hannon, did the saucer fly over?" said John with a knowing smile that needed no answer.

●◇ ◯◇ ●◇ ◯◇ ●◇ ◯◇ ●◇ ◯◇ ●◇

The Labour Exchange, as the employment office was known at the time, was down in Barry's Lane and a man called **Jimmy Aherne** was its manager. He was also the owner of Aherne's pub, which has now developed into a world famous hotel and restaurant. Jimmy was extremely shrewd. He could perform his duties as the manager of the Labour Exchange most discreetly without raising an eyebrow.

Having checked the signing-on list with **Sally and Paddy**, his clerks, he would slowly amble around town in a seemingly harmless manner, stopping here and there for a chat. A few words with **P.J. O'Gorman**, before a move on to **Jimmy McGuane, Flo Leahy** and **Michael Gould**. All were drapers, touching up their windows and hanging out their clothes, ready for customers' inspection. On the return walk Jimmy would saunter by the back streets and this was usually where his shrewdness would tell. Encountering an individual, who had signed on for unemployment assistance earlier, white-washing a wall for financial gain, Jimmy would walk over to admire the work. This, of course, was the last thing the lad wanted. "I think the colour is too plain," the manager would joke, "perhaps you could sign your name to it!" Message understood. That lad would never again work on a signing-on day.

◆ ○◆ ◆ ○◆ ◆ ○◆ ◆ ○◆ ◆ ◆

Jack Carey's forge was known far and wide throughout East Cork and West Waterford. Even in his so-called retirement, Jack was a great hand to shoe horses and he loved the fuss of being collected to be brought away to the stables of the big houses.

Jack is no longer with us, but a lot of what he told us will live on. I particularly remember when he mentioned about the old woman who lived in his area hundreds of years ago. She was able to foretell the future but mostly she was laughed at. One of her forecasts was that there would be a large settlement at Ballydaniel, halfway between Tallow and Youghal. This sounded incredible as the towns are only thirteen miles apart. Then, in penal times, with so many evictions, the misfortunate homeless people began to gather near Ardagh graveyard at Ballydaniel.

There arose a large shanty town of cabins, where hundreds of people existed, while deciding their future. The old woman had been right.

●◇ ◌◈ ●◇ ◌◈ ●◇ ◌◈ ●◇ ◌◈ ●◇

Richard (Dick) Griffin ran a grocery shop, with his wife **Pauline**, at the top of Brown Street. He was a kind gentle soul, full of good humour. I would say that he never raised his voice in anger at anybody and the following example gives testimony to his patience and tact: Dick was measuring behind the shop counter for some new shelving while Pauline was serving the customers. He was on his knees, quietly writing down figures and could not be seen from outside the counter. In came a woman with a child in a pram to make a few purchases. She asked for Rinso, which was up on the high shelf and so Pauline had to get the stool to reach it. The customer saw her chance and behind Pauline's back, grabbed a pound of sausages and stuffed them under the blanket in the pram beside the baby. She then asked for Fry's cocoa, up high at the other side. Again, Pauline was distracted in reaching up and the woman put two rings of black pudding under the blanket in the pram.

Dick could see all this through a crack in the front of the counter and when the customer requested another item which was high up, Dick suddenly stood up, giving the woman a fright saying "Mam, if you put any more food into that pram, you'll suffocate the baby."

The practice of capturing and trading in songbirds was widespread before the coming of radio and television. It was common to see local characters heading for the country, with cages and cribs, to seek out the finches and linnets. Cribs were basin-like traps made of light twigs and could be knocked down over the unsuspecting bird by pulling a string or by a trigger-twig which the bird would stand on. An already caged bird would sometimes be brought along to attract the wild one with his singing and a few pieces of bread in the crib would bring him the rest of the way.

●◇ ◌◈ ●◇ ◌◈ ●◇ ◌◈ ●◇ ◌◈ ●◇

In towns and cities, you would find cages of birds hanging outside houses in lanes, courts, alleys and streets. On fine days, birds were singing everywhere. An orchard-type air gave gaiety to those narrow passages. Usually over doorways and windows the cages were placed to enable the house owner to hear the singing and also to keep an eye on the cages. It was considered good fun for a character to quickly swop cages, leaving a bad singer in place of a great one. If the owner missed the switch, he could spend days wondering how his great singer had lost his voice.

Dinny O'Brien-Stokes was a great judge of a songbird. Many are the stories told about him and at this late stage, one can hear as many versions of the same story. Dinny was a painter and general worker and the priests in town always enjoyed his wit as he did the odd jobs for them. However, the irregular availability of work coupled with the Irish weather led to an erratic income from the jobs, so he earned a few bob with the cages for his 'black nourishment' in slack times.

He is said to have approached a Fr. O'Connor on the street saying that he had something to confess. "Ah! Not here!" said the priest. "This is not the place." Dinny raised his voice with excitement and he gasping for a pint. "I must tell you now," said Dinny. "I went to bed last night and forgot to water the birds." The priest gave a sigh of relief. It was not so bad. "That's alright," said the priest. "That's no harm." "Ah! but," said Dinny, "I woke at three in the morning and because all the taps were frozen, I had no water. All I had was a bottle of Knock water and God forgive me, Father, didn't I give them the Holy water."

"Okay," said Fr. O'Connor, "It's still not too bad." "And then," said Dinny, "at seven o'clock this morning, they woke me like a choir, singing, 'Faith of our Fathers.'" The priest gave a loud laugh. "Well done Dinny. Here's a half-crown for a few pints." Dinny had entertained the man so well that he parted with the coin painlessly.

While helping the priest at his house in Emmet Place, Dinny had reason to move a few bags of empty altar-wine bottles. A fair thirst was on him as he eyed the bottles anxiously. Fr. O'Connor copped him and quickly remarked, "Don't mind those, Dinny, they're all dead men."

"If they are," Dinny replied, "I don't think they died without the priest."

On another occasion, he was passing by the Parish Church as two old women came out after the evening devotions. Dinny had a few pints in him and was swaggering a bit. "Look at him," said one woman to the other. "Isn't drink an awful cross?"

"That's right," answered Dinny. "And the Lord said, "Take up your cross and follow me."

Dinny's fame brought him many sales. A woman from the Strand sent word that she wanted to buy a really good singer for big money. Dinny was delighted, but he only had one good singer at that time. This bird, he was really keeping for himself, but the woman had plenty of money. Out went the bird in his cage to the strand and proceeded to transform the whole area by attracting many other singers.

Then while the new owner and a neighbour were admiring the bird, he fell off the perch and landed on the floor of the cage. They stood him back up but after a few minutes singing, he fell off the perch again. On examining the bird, they discovered that he had only one leg. Hell hath no fury like a woman scorned! "You cheated me!" she roared. "That bird has only one leg!'

"Ah! now, Mam,' said Dinny. "You ordered a singer, not a dancer!"

The next morning, being Sunday, Dinny was at 12 o'clock Mass and when it finished he walked down to wait outside Finn's pub. It was near to opening time and he had plenty of company at Meat Shambles Lane Corner, all knowing that the woman from the Strand had parted with big money. When the door opened, Dinny was first through and waved back to the crowd to follow him. Needless to say, there was a rush and in a few seconds, the place was full. Dinny told the publican to stand drinks to two of the crowd, to the consternation of all the rest.

"Come on, Dinny," they chorused. "You called us all in."

"Now, now," said Dinny. "Were ye at Mass today? Did ye hear the priest? Many are called, but few are chosen.!"

No doubt about it, but Dinny was the Brendan Behan of Youghal. He was witty, funny, liked his pint and even composed

*William Swayne and John Casey receive their prizes
after a good day's fishing.*

poetry. Sadly, he didn't write it down and no acquaintance of h.
did either. A terrible loss. Only now are the pieces being put
together and the gaps are enormous. At least some of his better
stories are recorded.

Canon Dineen was looking for a nice songbird and of course
contacted Dinny. Sixpence was charged for the bird and the
Canon went happily away. After a week, he was back complaining
that the bird was a poor singer.

"What do you expect for sixpence, John McCormack?" was
Dinny's reply.

A shoemaker traded with Dinny, promising a pair of boots for
a songbird. The bird was handed over but the boots were never
produced in return. In spite of that, the shoemaker still found the
nerve to complain to Dinny that the bird wasn't singing.

"Hold on, could it be that his boots are too tight for him?"
said Dinny.

Before we leave the songbird era, let me introduce two more
characters. **Dick Torpey**, of North Main Street and **Johnny
Murray** from Knockanore. Two great story-tellers they were and
the 'taller' the better. Down on the quayside, sitting on the seats
with all the old tars listening, they would try to better each other.

The town man, Dick Torpey, liked to do a little bird-catching
and he put down his crib one day, near the top of Cork Hill. It
was a self-activating one and having set and baited it, he left for
home.

A few local lads were passing by after a fishing session at the
quayside. They saw Dick departing from the crib and decided to
play a trick on him. One small flat fish that they didn't want was
thrown into the crib. So what you had was - a flatfish in a bird
trap at the top of Cork Hill.

The next day Johnny Murray was in town and was holding the
attention of all as he told his latest story. "I went out this morning
at ten o'clock to my orchard and saw a blackbird just starting to
eat one of my huge apples. Going out again at twelve o'clock, I
found the blackbird inside the apple. All I could see was his tail."

"top!" said Dick Torpey. "I put down my bird-crib at Cork Hill last evening and there was such a high tide that when I went back this morning, there was a flat aught in it!"

●◇ ◇● ●◇ ◇● ●◇ ◇● ●◇ ◇● ●◇

Jack Sullivan's barber shop at North Main Street was a great place for a haircut, shave, chat and sit down. It was just for males, in those years after the war, long before unisex hair salons came to Irish towns. Men from the country would love to sit patiently along the hard wooden benches around the walls as they listened to all the news. Their people at home would expect the latest in chat from the town on the men's return, and this was one of the best places to hear it.

The barber shop was just one of the rest places in town for a visitor. Public houses and eating houses were also patronised as places of rest and refreshment.

Jack was a great talker himself and was prone to get completely carried away on the subject of pigeons. You see, he was a keen breeder, racer and follower of these special birds. Just imagine then, when another pigeon fancier sat on the chair for a trim. Everything, except the chat, would proceed in slow motion as the races from as far away as Scotland were detailed.

During one of those long chin-wags, a man from County Waterford was sitting in the queue on the wall-to-wall timber seating. For ages, he just listened and listened until he felt they would never stop, so he gave out. "Ah, come on, we'll be here all day." A silence followed that could be weighed! Jack looked sideways at the intruder out of the corner of his eye but didn't say anything. When the Waterford man's turn came, he asked for a shave and Jack proceeded to lather his face up well. Then, a little way through the process, with just the locks shaved, Jack announced that he was going into the kitchen for his tea. The client was livid, as he sat there on the barber's chair, covered in soapy foam. Time passed, ten minutes became twenty with no sign of Jack returning. The customer had enough! He whipped off the white bib and in spite of his ridiculous facial appearance,

28

charged out of the premises. Across the road, he ran to Jim McCarthy's pub for a drink.

The barman put a big frothy pint on the counter in front of him. At that moment, two strangers came into the pub and one said to the other, "There's a great pint in this house." The client looked up from the glass at the newcomers. "Look at him," they chorused "there's a great frothy pint in this house."

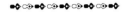

Side cars pulled by ponies were the forerunner to the Hackney cars or Taxis as we now know them. They would be hired for short journeys to the railway or for the trip out the country on a fine day. Near the Strand in Youghal, lived an old very cute side-car operator and his favourite stand was at the local railway station. He would canvas for business on the platform, hoping to get a long journey. "Side car for hire," he was shouting as the train arrived one summer's morning. "Distance no object," said he hopefully. An American tourist and his wife approached the jarvey. He was anxious to get their heavy cases on board before any discussion about destination or fee. So on went the cases and up sat the visitors. The jarvey could now smile. "Where to, folks?" he asked. "Atlantic Hotel, please," said the visitors. The driver nearly fell off the side car, because the Atlantic Hotel was only a hundred yards away on the hillside overlooking the station. "Keep cool now," whispered the jarvey to himself as he faced away from the requested destination to commence a detour. He started to tell stories and went on to amuse them so much that they were won over completely by his charm. Out the Front Strand they went, on to Claycastle, over the Railway Bridge and back in the Killeagh Road to the Atlantic Hotel. Never once did they suspect that he was cheating them. The next morning when the American lady pulled back the curtains of their front bedroom in the hotel, she discovered a view of the railway station. Still not doubting the jarvey, she turned around to her husband. "Fred, we got off at the wrong station, there's another one just below.

Let me tell a story about a C.I.E. delivery man named **Jack Browne** who worked with a great shire horse and cart delivering barrels of stout to the public houses in the town. The relationship between the man and horse was remarkable. This could be attributed not only to the many hours, six days a week, spent working together, but to the care that Jack and his brother Michael gave to their two railway horses. The men were also grooms to the horses - watering, feeding, stabling and brushing them. When going from pub to pub, Jack would never ride on the cart and so there was no need for the reins. When he walked up the street the horse would follow, pulling the cart out from the kerb neatly and slipping in at the next pub perfectly. The horse liked a drink of porter from a bucket as a reward but never, though merry, did he misjudge his loaded cart.

Jack Browne and Jerry Kelly, loading the last railway horses to work the streets

●◇ ◑◇ ●◇ ◑◇ ●◇ ◑◇ ●◇ ◑◇ ●◇

Bachelors were forever goading each other to get married as a kind of 'craic' and this was very widespread in country areas. A few miles outside Youghal a group of them would gather at the crossroads, in the summer evenings, to play pitch and toss with ha'pennies, while speculating on each other's marriage prospects. In this particular group, the ages averaged from about twenty to thirty-five years, with a big exception, one of the bachelors was seventy years old. Yes, a mere seventy, and he with all the talk and notions. But, stop! He found himself a wife before anybody else and they were speechless, dumbfounded! They could not believe it. The *old fella* was getting married and the date was set.

The marriage took place in the local Parish Church and afterwards the groom took his new wife and their few relations down town to a local eating house. Then it was home to the country with his bride. He had been living alone and so there was no complication. The kettle was put on the big roaring fire and they seemed to be blissfully alone. That is except for the young bachelors who were climbing on to the roof to play a trick on the lovebirds.

When they judged that the couple had gone off to bed, a sod was put on top of the chimney, blocking it. It wasn't long before the house began to fill with smoke causing the groom to run out in his nightshirt to be greeted by a big cheer. Again the bride ran out coughing and spluttering in her nightie to another big cheer.

The following morning the bride was in town to do her shopping, when she met a pal of hers. This friend could not have heard anything about the sod on the chimney but she was aware of the age of the new husband. "How did it go?" said the pal. "Were the fires of love burning last night?" "They were," said the bride. "Sure hadn't we to run out of the house from the smoke!"

Billy Swayne – Storyteller Supreme!
Photograph by Padraig Ó Flannabhra AIPPA

➡️◦➡️◦➡️◦➡️◦➡️◦➡️

Dan Duskey was a showman with a small travelling outfit of his own, going from village to village in the earlier part of this century. His wife Peggy, sons and daughters, made up the cast.

There are many stories about the hard-working Dan and his show while touring around the South of Ireland. He arrived in Clashmore village in West Waterford before the war with a van pulling a wagon. His theatre at the time was an all-canvas one and had seen its best days years before that. Dan was undeterred. It was all that he had and he set up just below the bridge.

A few people ventured in to see the first night's performance and test the talent. They were the 'experts' who would not miss a show of any kind. A travelling troupe could be accepted, or quickly dismissed, on the reports of the critics. After the show, one would hear, "How was it? Are they good? Are they funny?" and the inquest went on, amongst those sitting on the bridge, late into the night. Back at the show, the entertainers, having done their utmost, were going to bed and hopes were high of getting good reports. It would mean a few weeks of regular income and stability of life. No pulling down the tent, no travelling and no re-erecting in the immediate future. More importantly, a chance for the children to attend school and make friends with other kids. Shops to be familiar with, people to smile at and a community to belong to, if only for a month of so.

The feed-back was good and the attendances improved - the show was accepted! The energy saved through not moving on was then put into rehearsals every afternoon, to ensure the freshness of change. Survival demanded that the small population did not get bored and this was uppermost in the performers' minds. So a different programme was needed nightly. Eventually, the fear of staleness led on to the local talent contests. Locals were now entertaining themselves with the means and encouragement coming from the professionals. Remarkably, the audiences at the talent shows often surpassed in number those for the regular shows. Mothers, fathers, brothers and sisters would pour in from the surrounding countryside to see their Paddy, and of course, in their eyes, he was great. Talent contests had a funny habit like that of discovering hidden wonders. For the final, a judge from some other parish would be invited to do the honours. Then, if the favourite didn't win, the harmony of the village would not be upset. It could, however mean the prompt despatch of the road show, but it made no difference now. Time to move on regardless!

Another village, new faces! Another school, new teachers!

During the Second World War, Duskey Dan, like all civilians, could not get petrol for his van, so a donkey and dray were bought to bring the gear from place to place. On steep hills, the animal would be helped by Dan to pull up the load. This was done by tying a strong rope on to the shafts and Dan would walk ahead of the donkey pulling the rope over his shoulder.

A postman called **Tom Bagg** came across this scene on Lickey Hill near Piltown, as Dan was assisting the donkey.

"That's a great animal that you have there," said Tom.

"He's not as good as the other donkey!" said the showman.

"What other donkey?"

"The two-legged donkey in front of him!" said Duskey Dan.

It was during a return visit to Clashmore that the show got a great shot in the arm from **Michael Kenure**, a local merchant. A very appreciative and charitable man was the same Michael. He had realised how hard Dan worked to keep his head above water and how much the show meant to the morale of the villagers. Performances were at this time being held in an all-canvas marquee which was extremely old. Michael Kenure went to Cork where he bought new canvas, brought it home and presented it to Duskey Dan. By way of Dan's appreciation, the first show under the new cover was admission free. Tears of happiness were in Dan's eyes that night as he thanked profoundly his benefactor and the people of the village of Clashmore for their tremendous support and friendliness.

The show then moved to Youghal where a large number of soldiers were stationed for the Emergency. Every performance was packed full. The town had two cinemas and several dance halls but the live show of the Duskeys got more than its share of the army pay packets. So successful was it that a local man, Mickey McCarthy, was hired to play his accordion as support music for the acts.

Dan's next stop was at Ballymacoda where more soldiers were

billeted. Again, great attendances every night and many very hard-working but enjoyable weeks were spent there.

Years later, the Duskeys managed to buy a hippodrome booth which had solid timber sides with a canvas roof. The new 'house' was safer and more secure on windy nights, easier to heat and generally a lot more cosy. It meant that the show could go on almost regardless of the weather and the showman's income became a bit more consistent.

Dan's later years were not spent in our area, but no doubt his great will-power saw him survive. Maybe one day, when his energy diminished and the uncertainty, anxiety and hardship could be taken no longer, Dan Duskey retired. I hope so. He deserved it.

A typical entertaining character was the famous **Jim Whyte** of Mill Road. He could conjure up innocent fun from every day life with an alertness that was contradictory to his easy-going look. Especially in the company of fellow funsters, he would blossom forth, creating humour as he spoke. **Philly Bride, Billy O'Connell** and **Terry Butler** were some of his pals. Jim would have them laughing so much that their pints of porter would last for ages.

"Stop! Hold your tongue! The pints are going flat," they would plead.

He would have some smart remark to answer that, like, "Ye shouldn't get any more drink, ye're too giddy already."

One day Jim walked into Paddy Maher's pub and gave a shout to the six men at the counter. "Drink up those pints fast."

Thinking that he was going to 'stand' them, they quickly emptied their glasses. "Come on, we're going for a walk," said Jim. That was one day when he was the only one to laugh.

A sad story from Mill Road concerns a youthful **Johnny Kenefick** who, as a rebel, was on the run and could not spend a night at home for fear of capture. In those difficult Black and Tan years, all residents of a house had to be listed after curfew. Then, if the soldiers raided they knew how many people should be inside.

Johnny Kenefick slept where he could. It is said that men often slept over the kilns in the Brickyard for the heat during the bad winter nights. Eventually, the hard life caught up with Johnny. He became ill with pneumonia, needed nursing badly, but could not go home. **Mrs. Kenna**, a neighbour and good friend, took him in to nurse him. She lived with her brother who was prone to wander to other houses, even after curfew, to play cards. Somebody must have been talking because Mrs. Kenna's house was raided two nights later and fortunately the brother was visiting a few doors away. There being two occupants listed for the house, the woman pretended that the man in the bed was her brother, thereby saving Johnny's life.

After the truce, Johnny Kenefick stood as a candidate for the Urban District Council and was elected. But the joy of his success was short-lived, as his chest trouble developed into terminal tuberculosis. A sad loss, at thirty-four years of age, to his ageing parents, young brothers and sisters.

At that time, a corpse was waked at home before the funeral took place from the house directly to the graveyard. It was on the 15th June 1922 that the pipe band played the remains of Johnny Kenefick the short distance from his home in Mill Road to North Abbey.

A view of the Clockgate from the Jail Steps Laneway

A THRESHING DAY IN WEST WATERFORD

The big steam engine dominated all other activity in the country as it built up power in readiness for a busy day. Such a lovely sight, so clean, so colourful and the brass shining in the early morning of a lovely September day.

"Fáilte roimh gach éine", said the farmer as he greeted all the neighbours and friends who had kindly and voluntarily come to help. All were well rested after an early night in bed in readiness for the day.

Terms like *community cooperation* were unknown to those hard-working people but their behaviour spoke louder than any big words. Every man would bring his pike and every woman would help in the kitchen. There were a few certainties about the day - plenty of hard work, great craic and loads to eat and drink. There would definitely be no hunger!

Summer had been fairly fine with good heat and the corn was promising. Just to look at that great big reek was to wonder if it could be done in one day. But many hands make light work, they were here in strong numbers and all were used to good hard labour. No soft fleshy hands on this lot! Six days a week in the fields and prising the thorns out of the fingers on Sunday.

Steam up, the drive belt on, a sharp blow of the whistle for good luck, and the work would start.

It is after eight o'clock and there is corn to be piked. Sheaf after sheaf is heaved into the the threshing machine. Straw is flying out on to the ground and the chaff is everywhere. A big cheer for the first bagful! Those sacks must be over a hundredweight. Time flies and soon there is 'tae' on offer or if preferred, a pint of loose porter. Most of the men take the porter. A great thirst is on them and the black liquid wets their moustaches as they take big gulps. Interesting to see all the caps now worn back to front, with the peak covering the neck from the sun. Braces are everywhere, worn over heavy white shirts, grey with age. Not a collar or stud to be seen.

The shirts of years ago had detachable collars, which could be washed separately, thereby saving labour at the washboard. Men shaved and washed with their shirts on and put on the collar, which was attached with a stud at the front, just before going out.

An old character, who was not famous for cleanliness, was preparing to go out when he was heard to say, "I wonder will I put on my collar or wash my neck?"

Back to the threshing - trousers are either wool or corduroy, loose and baggy, resting on fine heavy leather boots. An old saying was "If you want to remain healthy, keep your head and feet warm." With their caps and boots on, they've all heard that.

A couple of hours later, the Angelus bell rings out from the village church over the countryside and the workers stop to say the prayers. Caps come off and the heads are bowed for a short few moments, then smiles spread all over the weather-beaten faces to reveal good teeth, bad teeth, and in some faces - no teeth! It is time for dinner. There are ten chairs around the huge kitchen table and another six at the parlour table in *the room*. In a few houses, the farmers would be directed to the parlour but the labourers stayed in the kitchen. Spuds on a corn sack in the middle of the table are piled high and your plate is filled with bacon and cabbage. Then, to wash it all down, what else but

Reaping and Binding at Shanacoole, Jer and Dan O'Shea

more from the barrel of loose porter?

Pig's head and cabbage was always a farmhouse favourite and would at times be provided for the hard-working men at threshings. Tasty and chewy would be a good description of it.

It was while chewing on a piece of pig's head that one man felt a long thin stick in his mouth. It seemed like a matchstick, but on pulling it from between his teeth, he discovered it to be a darning needle. Wonder of wonders! How did a needle get into a pig's cheek? Just then, the woman of the house owned up and claimed to darn by the fireside at night and would use the pigs' heads, smoking over the fireplace, as handy pin cushions.

The local postman walks in with a letter. Even though busy, she greets him with her warm welcome and tells him to sit down at his usual place. After all, she says, he is a daily caller. But the quiet postman stands against the wall waiting for someone to finish. The *Bean an Ti* spots him and quickly evicts a hard-working man with meat in his mouth from the postman's place at table. As the unfortunate pikeman stands against the wall, trying to swallow his food, the red-faced postman sits down.

The bacon at this threshing today was tasty and well cooked and not like further out the hills last year when the meat was tough and only half-cooked. On that occasion, one character remarked that when he noticed the sheepdog was fat, he knew that the grub was suspect because the dog was getting most of it. At the dinner that day, the men were unable to chew the bacon and passed lumps of it to the dog under the table, hoping to save face with the cook. But even the dog didn't eat it and it was left strewn there on the floor. The character gave up and there and then wrote a poem about it.

O Lord above
look down with love
And have pity on us four,
Send us *mate*
that we can ate
and take away the boar.

Back to work - piking, tossing and bagging. A bit of stiffness after the dinner sit-down but ten minutes later all joints are smoothly moving again. The reek is now shrinking and the heads of the pikemen on the far side can be seen. One would expect that the older men would tire first, but this is not so. They are the methodical men, working steadily.

Earlier in the day, the fit young men felt that they could go on forever, but this is a game of judgement and the evenly paced man lasts willingly to the end of a hard day. All the corn is threshed by six o'clock. Time for the *tae*. A big fry-up of rashers, sausages, eggs and the left-over potatoes followed by chunks of hot curranty bastible cake with lumps of butter melting on it. "Pour the loose porter for those thirsty men," says the woman.

Darkness is creeping over the haggard as the first workers depart for home. Others will stay for *the craic* and the story-telling. Maybe the box (melodeon) will be brought out and a half-set danced by the few with some energy left.

The steam engine is silent in the moonlight with the thresher motionless beside it. Their work is done for another day. Early tomorrow morning, the show moves along the hill road to the next farmer and the workers will go with it. But tonight is for rest as some men bed down in the nice warm chaff under the thresher. It's a hard and great life.

Threshing at Shanacoole, Peg O'Shea & Jim Ledingham

THE FERRYBOAT

The Ferry, Youghal.

Travelling down the Lighthouse Hill towards town, a glance across the river shows the lovely Monatrea Headland. Although seemingly so near across the water, overland it is eight miles to town by a horseshoe of roads. So it was, before motor transport, when people walked and cycled, that the ferryboat service did great business. It ran from a little jetty on the north side of the ferry point to the ferry slip near Market Square in town, and for years the fare was just fourpence return. People from places like Piltown, Whiting Bay and even Ardmore would walk to the point to embark for the few minutes crossing to the heart of Youghal. They felt part of the town, so reliable and regular was the ferryboat. The fact that they belonged to a different parish and even to a different county was forgotten in the quick boat trip across the river. Bags of messages (shopping) and even bikes were carried in the big open boats.

As transport in motor cars and motor bikes became common in the 1950s, the passenger number on the ferry began to drop until, in 1959, it ceased operations.

The Youghal U.D.C. ran the service as far back as I can

remember with two boats, the Angeline and the Rosaline. Mr. James Smyth of the Brickyard was Chairman of the U.D.C. and the boats were called after his daughters. Excursions up-river as far as Cappoquin were given in summer which were very attractive for the holiday-makers. The Blackwater was called the Irish Rhine because of its resemblance to that great continental waterway with miles of wooded hillside and numerous castles. Places like the Knights Templars fortress at Rhincrew, Templemichael Castle, Molana Island Abbey, Ballynatray Great House (said to have a window for every day in the year), Old and New Strancally Castles and Dromanna Castle are dotted along the banks for the first few miles.

In Hayman's Annals of Youghal, there is a short mention of a ferryboat sinking in 1876 with the loss of fourteen lives and more being saved. Following up on that, Johnny Veale of Springfield Monatrea, was able to give some details. It seems that a youth from Aglish had brought corn to the Piltown Mill for grinding and while waiting, he decided to take the ferry to town to pass away a few hours. On the return journey, the boat sank and he was drowned.

In earlier times the Blackwater tourist steamship *Ness Queen* under the management of Michael Kennedy, plied the river and a timetable for the summer months was posted in hotels and railways stations to publicise the daily sailings. Because the river is tidal to Villierstown, which is most of the journey to Cappoquin, departure times varied with the tides.

You had the first and second class fares, single and return, to chose from on the regular daily service, while excursion day rates were all by second class fee. Dogs were one shilling and bicycles ninepence.

Shops and pubs in the Market Square, all did well from the ferry passengers. Naturally enough, the bags of messages were purchased nearby to save lugging them too far. Likewise for the pubs, as people had a drink or two while they waited for the ferry bell to summon them. Miss Dunny's, Brennan's, O'Gorman's, Turner's Ferry Bar and Paddy Linehan's (later to become Moby Dick's) were the scenes of the *craic* before the crossing back to West Waterford. Dunny's was very near the slipway/ferry office and Johnny Dunny would play the melodeon for the singsong. Then Bong! Bong! Bong!, the bell would ring out and the ballad would be finished on the boat.

Before we leave Dunny's pub, a tale concerning some local fishermen tells of Miss Dunny and friends walking home from Mass at the Presentation Convent Church on a Sunday morning. Passing by the Mall House (Town Hall), they came upon some fishermen drinking from a barrel of loose porter which they had nicely positioned on the low wall. All of the previous week, the weather had been very bad and of course the morale of the men was low. They said a kind benefactor had given them a barrel to cheer them up. The old women, together with Miss Dunny, wished them well. 'God bless the doner,' said Miss Dunny and her friends, as the fishermen smiled and drank away. That was okay until Miss Dunny, having had her breakfast, went out to the pub store in the back yard to check her stock for the day. A barrel was missing! And to think that they had her good wishes as well!

1954 saw the making of the Moby Dick classic at the Market Quay and dock. Tall ships seemed to be everywhere. Some were genuine, like the featured Peaquod and the James Apostlewaite, but in other cases, it was just big poles stuck in the ground, rigged out like masts.

A visiting B.B.C television crew, over here in connection with the film, decided to make a special show featuring the ferryboat with the local choir. Fr. Barry, fondly called P. de B. was the choirmaster of the youthful singers and his favourite saying was, "I'm trying to give you something that you will have for the rest of your life - an appreciation of good music." Practises were held every Tuesday and Friday after school in the League of the Cross Hall. How we loved when Fr. Barry was on sick calls and prayed that he would get a call so we could go home. It was a fair achievement to shape teenagers like us into a four-part choir. Fr. Barry, by arrangement with the B.B.C. team, brought the choir across on the ferryboat to Monatrea from where we walked to Whiting Bay for a picnic. Or so we thought! We were only a short time at the beach when a blackboard was produced and we found ourselves learning 'Eilín a Rún' in four parts.

Coming back on the boat, we were taken down river, instead

of across it. Passing the Green Park wall, we were singing the song just learned on the picnic, and unknown to us, the cameras were filming from shore. People thronged the sea wall along by the Lighthouse and out the promenade to get a look at this choir on water. It was a lovely summer's evening and the still water easily carried the singing ashore. As we alighted back at the quay, we felt like film stars and had to walk up the slipway many times before we got it right for the cameras.

One pilot of the ferry service stands out in memory and he was Moss Geary of Windmill Hill. A very dignified old man, smoking his pipe like a sea captain, is how younger people remember him. He was perfect for the part.

Moss Geary in action with Billy Ahern at the wheel

A SEA TRAGEDY

The schooner William S. Green was built at Bideford in 1858 by John Johnson and was registered at Cork. She was 93 tons with dimensions of 77.5' X 20.3' X 10.4'. While operating out of Youghal carrying the F for Farrell houseflag, she was lost with all hands in February 1904 off the Devon coast.

Normally, the vessel carried three of a crew with the captain, and on that last voyage the sailors were: **Captain Jack O'Loughlin, Jim O'Loughlin, Michael Walsh & Dan Coakley.** As in most major calamities, there was a hard luck story and a good luck one associated with this loss. **Billaboy Coakley** was a regular crew member of the William S. Green, but because his wife was about to give birth, he stayed at home from this voyage. His brother, Dan, went instead to keep the crew-place in the family, and it cost him his life. In contrast, while the schooner was docked in Cardiff, Jim O'Loughlin developed a poisoned hand which prevented him from leaving with the ship and so his life was spared.

The William S. Green left Cardiff the evening before the disaster in smooth seas with the wind west south-west. She carried a cargo of coal, flour and bran, and was bound for Youghal. At the same time, another vessel Deigratia also left to make the same journey. Both ships were driven by sail and had to short tack into the wind. As they sailed down the Bristol Channel, they were seen at 6.30 in the evening, ten miles southwest of Colney Island. Rough seas were now coming up.

The Deigratia made for and got shelter in Milford Haven. The William S. Green was not so lucky and she was enveloped in the heavy mist. On the starborard tack on the flood tide, she went ashore on the rocks in Bideford Bay.

Sophie Murphy as a young girl was standing at her doorway in North Main Street on the night of 18th February 1904. She saw the figure of Danny Coakley come into North Main Street from the quayside via Meatshambles Lane. Danny's house was just next door to Sophie's and she said "Goodnight, Danny", as he went in home. To her consternation Mrs. Coakley denied the

The making of 'Moby Dick' in 1954
Note the masts sticking out of solid ground on the right-hand side of the timber house.
Photo – Cork Examiner

Characters Galore!

Paddy Linehan and his wife Maureen behind their bar in 1955.
The customers are Cecil Pratt, Billy O'Connell, Johnny Buttimer and Ken Parker
A few years later, this pub was transformed to become 'Moby Dicks', named after the famous film.

next morning that her son had come home and was not due for another few days. The following weeks brought the realisation that Danny Coakley would never again come home in the flesh. But who knows? Was Sophie right? Did Danny come home in spirit on that fateful February night?

The following are details from the Bideford Gazette concerning the tragedy: On February 19th, 1904, at about 6 o'clock at that Saturday morning, a coastguard on duty at Downend near Croyde saw a dismasted ship on the rocks nearby. She was subsequently found to be the Willam S. Green, owners Thomas and Farrell, on a voyage from Cardiff to Youghal. There was no sign of life, and the ship's boat was on the rocks near the vessel.

The inquest was told that the weather was a mixture of heavy mist and driving rain with short visibility. The coastguards in their station, just 100 yards from the wreck, had not seen distress signals, but then they could only see Bull Point Light at intervals that night. It was thought at the time that four men had perished, but with Jim O'Loughlin in a Cardiff hospital, there were just three on board. Two bodies were washed ashore and were buried at Barnstaple. God rest all their souls. And so the William S. Green, launched at Bideford in 1858, was to return to the same area to meet its death on the nearby rocks a mere 46 years later.

THE COUNTRY POSTMAN TO GORTROE

On church Holy Days, the country postman faced a much different day to normal.

During the sorting of the mail, the country postman would noticeably rush through his work - no talk, no distraction - but full of concentration. On Holy Days he prepared differently. Instead of many bundles of letters, he made just two large ones. The rush was for the 9.30 a.m. Mass in the small church (Church of Ease) on his route. Thus the two bundles - one for Mass time delivery and the other for the remainder.

Out the road, he is like the Sí Gaoithe, a letter in here and there. 'Good morning and good luck,' as he burns up the miles.' Get me to the Church on time'' seems to be his song this morning. Cycling into the church grounds, he jumps off the bike and, using his mailbag as a ram, he pushes into the last-in first-out crowd gathered in the porch. From then, he is tormented by people gesturing to him, looking for a signal as to whether their cheque or important letter has come.

Many the new priest thought that the postman had some nervous disorder as he kept winking, blinking, nodding and shaking his head in all directions, during the whole of Mass. Very distracting - half the congregation anxious and the other half curious! The priest was not happy and the postman likewise - this could not go on. The problem was solved on the next Holy Day by the shrewd postman. He walked up the aisle to the top pew and there he deposited himself with the bag of post. Perfect peace! A devout congregation! Even those who would normally leave early, stayed on, eyeing the postman's every move as they witnessed and experienced a piece of the Mass that was new to them.

He stayed on to say a few prayers for the holy souls after the priest left the altar and still he was undisturbed. Nobody talked or even whispered in the Church. It seemed an age before he blessed himself and made his exit, to be mobbed outside. "I've

never seen the complete attendance to wait on like that before,"
said the priest. "Any chance that you could do it for me on
Sundays?" Ten minutes later, the remaining post was easy to
count. Yes, home early today! Then change clothes and a walk
downtown - just like the country people on a Holy day. And why
not? He was a country postman.

KINSALEBEG POST OFFICE

For many years, at Kinsalebeg, in Co. Waterford, two sisters, **Nora** and **Mary-Ann O'Shea** ran a shop and post office which was delightfully part of the last century in presentation and administration. Although they were in business until the 1970s, the premises was as it stood in the 1800s. The roof was thatched and had small windows set in thick walls. Inside, the timber shelves were sectioned off to keep the Sunlight Soap apart from the bread and the Fry's cocoa away from the Science boot polish.

The boarded timber ceiling was a mass of small hooks from which hung bunches of odds and ends, any of which could mean salvation to a country home in the middle of winter. You had primus needles, mantles, pipe covers, pipe cleaners, safety pins, oil lamp wicks, studs for shirt collars, shoe horns and studs for boots. Some hard working people wore loose leather or rubber boots during the week, but when Sunday Mass time arrived, they had to get the shoe horn to get their feet into the tidier shoes. Bootlaces and shoelaces, jars of buttons, the Macs Smile blades next to the Rinso soap powder. Add to all that the usual foodstuffs

John Forrest

like butter, tea, sugar, biscuits and jams, a few Mass cards, hankies, socks, women's head squares, brushes, candles and newspapers. Throw in a Post Office and you have the support for the parish, open all day, every day, Sunday included.

It was here that a batchelor farmer came to buy his groceries. Like a lot of people at the time, brand names and packaging meant nothing to him. One of his shopping visits was recorded as "Give me something to wash me clothes, and while you're at it, give me something to wash meself!" Absolute faith in the storekeeper. Customers could call at 8 a.m. for the paper and be back at 11 p.m. for the bread. Lots of country people preferred their bread 'cold' (one day old), to help prevent indigestion.

Nora was the Postmistress while Mary-Ann delivered the letters around the local seaside and headland. The post was done on a bike in all kinds of weather. Anybody who has lived a winter on a headland will know that when it blows and rains from the sea, shelter is scarce. The postwoman was tough and she wore her headscarf like a helmet, tied tightly under her chin with no hair or ears visible; just the little face with bright beady eyes shining out. Nora the clerk was programmed like a computer, before they were ever invented. She was so organised and had her area so regulated that there was a special day of the week for each type of post office transaction. When a person wanted to buy a dog licence or radio licence they were encouraged to come on a Monday. Tuesday was children's allowance day, Wednesday was usually the quietest day and anything awkward like insurance stamps, wet-time stamps and entertainment stamps were ordered and sold then. Thursday was posting day, to be delivered before the weekend. Pension day was Friday, while Saturday was children's day with savings stamps available.

In modern times, all of this sounds a bit incredible, but the people of that era were extremely happy with the service they got. A simple transaction could take up to a quarter of an hour. You would have the greeting, followed by the state of the weather, she would then commence the transaction and when completed, there would be a chat about the local news, and finally blessings and good luck on departure.

It was this postmistress, in her older years, who devised her own safety measures for balancing the Old Age Pension money, on a Friday morning, even before business commenced. She would receive the money from H.P.O. in £1 notes, 10 shilling notes and half-crowns. She would then, from memory, lay out all the individual amounts, and there were many different ones, along a shelf in readiness for collection. As each pensioner arrived, their bundle of money would be handed out, exactly correct to the last penny, from the shelf. There was never a shortage at the end of pension day.

Following a robbery on their premises in the 1960s, the sisters acquired a German Shepherd pup as a guard dog. A few months passed by, during which the guard dog became more and more of a pet, and he soon reached the size of a small donkey. I remember going in there a couple of times, to be pinned to the door by the huge friendly animal. He placed his paws on my shoulders and licked my face. When a person's arms are pinned back at the shoulders, his hands are pretty useless so the licking had to be endured. The postmistress would jump out from behind the counter. "Down boy, down boy! Sure he's only a pup!" The robbers must have got wind of the licking that they could be in for, as the two old ladies were never troubled again.

FAIR DAY IN A COUNTRY TOWN.

It is a dark, but dry, early morning, as the drover helps the farmer to move the twelve cattle out of the field into the boreen. The fair is fifteen miles away and there is road to be walked. Maybe 'to be run' would be a better expression, as the cattle move forward in fits and starts, running a mile, walking a mile, with the two men all the time in close attendance, keeping the animals to the far side of the road while passing a gap and then quickly heading them off at the crossroads further on.

The most difficult job of all was keeping apart from other herds as the activity increased getting nearer to the town. That specially kept cobblestone commonage in town called *The Fair Field* was half full before they got there at dawn. Over by the high wall at the back of the pub, they were lucky to get a sheltered place.

The cattle are easy to control now after a visit to the water trough, tired as they are, standing in a group. "I could do with a drop of Jameson," says the drover, as he makes for the nearby pub which has an exemption for the early arrivals. The sheep flocks are on the Main Street along the footpath about a yard apart with just a farmer or even a young boy - off school for the day - to attend to each lot. As for the dung on the ground, for those townies with shoes on, the only way to pass through the fair was to tip-toe down the middle of the road.

Pre-packed foods were only told of in faraway U.S.A., back in the 50s when the shops here cut rashers as ordered on a slicer and rows of pigs' heads looked out the window at the inches of dung outside. Whoever was sent to buy a pig's head was always asked not to go to a pub-grocery shop because the heads there never had any ears! Many years after, I found out why: the old men (some had been through the First World War) used to gather for a few pints and a smoke of the pipe. Pipe-smoking that time meant a plug of tobacco and a pen-knife to cut it with. When the barmaid would turn her back, the penknife would be used to cut an ear from the pig's head hanging overhead, and this would be chewed while drinking the porter.

Back at the fair - a 'jobber' approaches to admire the cattle and wishes "Good luck" for the day. The farmer is delighted; "a nice man," he thinks to himself. This middleman is a great judge of animals and the cattle exporters rely on him a lot for good stock. His good wishes so early is a good omen. Everybody knows that he earns his living making 'deals' between sellers and buyers. Back ambles the drover to give the farmer a break, enabling him to move around, meet some neighbours and admire the stock. The morning is passing without a bid. "Just keep calm!" Around the corner comes the jobber himself and with him a big cattle dealer. They whisper away to themselves before the dealer approaches to make an offer. It is a very bad offer.

"Take the cash and go home early," says the jobber, butting in. "You can't think of driving those cattle the fifteen miles home again," he teasingly suggests.

"No! No!" shouts the farmer, above the noise of the fair. "You're only a scoundrel!"

Muttering and shaking their heads, the cattle dealer and advisor vanish into the crowd.

The air calms down. Time for the Eating House (restaurant) and dinner.

Every 'digs' and tea-shop in the vicinity was open for meals on fair days and they were called Eating Houses (pronounced ateing). The grub was good, bacon and cabbage, plenty of it and all for a half-crown. This reminds me of the story about the farmer who was about to employ the labourer and he said, "I'll give you two pounds a week and 'ate' you (feed you) or I'll give you three pounds a week and you can 'ate' yourself!"

Back to the cattle - no sale yet, a little bit of anxiety creeps in, the afternoon is passing by. Plenty of room now on the cobblestones, several lots of cattle have changed hands and moved on in the last couple of hours. A few fellow farmers come along enquiring about the animals but they haven't the buying power of the big dealer-exporter. A local butcher wants to buy four of the animals at a good price and that, of course, would mean less to mind going home. Before the haggling with the butcher is finished, the jobber appears again and charges up to the farmer, closely followed by the dealer. "One last offer to you," he says, mentioning a price away above his earlier offer for the complete lot. The farmer is delighted but tries not to show it as the disappointed butcher moves away. "Shake hands on it, it's a deal!", declares the jobber as he stand between the dealer and the farmer like a referee in a boxing ring.

Money changes hands - all big notes - and the cattle are herded off to the railway wagons. A new view is now taken of the jobber. "A lovely man, there wouldn't be a fair at all without him," says the farmer to himself.

A successful Fair Day after all! Pay the drover, have a few pints and buy the groceries.

Then comes the easy part - a nice leisurely fifteen-mile walk home.

THE YOUGHAL STEAM LAUNDRY

Early this century, in a two-room cottage at Greencloyne Cross, the Wall family worked hard to make a success of their small laundry business. During those years, all the work was done by hand and was very laborious.

After a good soaking, the clothes were boiled in big buckets which were heated on small steel barrels of red coke from the Gas House. Sawdust, well-compacted by using the handle of a brush down through it to create an air hole, was also used in the barrels. Local sawmills like Murrays would give the sawdust free, just to have it taken away. Clothes were hand-washed, hung out to dry, brought in, ironed and folded without any mechanical help.

When large tubs of washing, in different stages of soakage, were placed on the roadside at Greencloyne, it was a sure sign that the weekend was nigh.

A family like the Walls - two parents and five children, would need every inch of that cottage, to eat together and relax on Sunday. So the laundry would be moved outdoors and what the small backyard did not hold was placed on the grass margin of Copperalley Road.

Staff of the Laundry with children Bernadette and Pauline McCarthy

Moll, Madge and **Annie** were the three daughters in the family and it was Moll, with her husband **Mick Lee** who decided to modernise. So, in 1916, the dream of a proper laundry was born. Mick had been in the Royal Irish Fusiliers and must have seen the likes of what he now had in mind on his many travels. He was determined that the work of the Laundry, as it now operated, could be made easier by modern methods.

A great friend of his was **James R. Smyth**, who was the Manager/Owner of the very successful Youghal Brickworks and a staunch believer in advancement by the use of latest developments. The Brickyard was already using a steam lorry to bring the bricks to the railway station, over three miles away. With the ambition of Mick teaming up with the experience of James R., the dream of a power-run laundry slowly took shape.

An aunt of the late John McCarthy, the blacksmith, was working in America during those years. Her name was **Bridget Crotty** and she was the owner of a piece of land which was directly across the North Road from the two-roomed house. Bridget agreed to give a site for the new project as she wisely foresaw that it would provide badly needed employment in the area.

A large timber structure, like a hall, was then built and the steam engine and fittings were bought in England and brought over. It was an instant success, giving employment to over thirty people in normal time, increasing to over forty in the summer. Those were the days when the 5,000 population of Youghal town would soar to a high of 15,000 during the August weekend.

Mick Lee himself would go in a horse van to the local strand to collect and deliver the clothes. He also travelled to Tallow, Lismore and Cappoquin, serving hotels, convents and institutions.

Coal and coke fired the furnace to make the steam, except during the Second World War when it ran on timber. As if to frustrate the Management at this time, the laundry got a large contract from the Army, thousands of whom were based at the Cork Hill Military Barracks for the *Emergency* years. Still the show went on.

On arrival, the dirty jumbled clothes were code-marked by hand with special ink before they were sorted into lots. *Marking* was a job more of checking than inking because the special ink usually outlived the life of the garment. Just new clothes, which had never been to the laundry before, had to be marked with the customer code number.

Steam power turned the big drive-shaft axles that ran across the roof of the building. Located on those were timber pulley wheels which drove the huge timber wash-tubs of clothes via thick leather belt connections.

Into the big tubs went the dirty linen to be tumbled by steam power for hundreds of revolutions accompanied by the remarkable liquid soap. Ha! you might say. 'Liquid soap, how are you?' There was no such thing, not even soap powder, and so it was concocted. The only soap available was in long brown bar form and was called *Tar Soap*. Many bars of this would be melted in a tank of water heated by steam and resulting in a kind of soap gel. A pint of this could shift tar, as the laundress would say. Tar was the problem stain on any white garment in those days.

After the washing would come the spinning and then it would be taken to the drying room. Here the clothes would be hung on lines in the warm air, again provided by the steam. Every housewife knows that a breath of the open air freshens clothes better than any drying room and so, on a fine day, line after long line of sheets could be seen billowing in the breeze beside the building.

Great steam presses ensured a smooth finish for the bigger pieces and when it came to ironing, there was no pause. An unusual centre-floor fire, fuelled by coke, housed a circle of solid hand irons. Around this at many tables, the ironing of shirts, collars and others was done. There were so many irons in the ring that when a worker found their one becoming cool, they simply replaced it and took another one. No delay!

Folding the many types of different garment was an art in itself. Each seemed to have its own distinctive presentation before the lot was documented, wrapped in brown paper and delivered with the invoice pinned to the top.

During the lifetime of the Youghal Steam Laundry, Mick Lee and his wife Moll made several purchases to update the plant and workings. A colander was bought to roll the sheets, dry them and neatly fold them. In the 1930s, a petrol lorry was purchased to speed up collection and delivery, and the 1950s saw the coke furnace converted to oil working. Sadly, the laundry closed in July 1962 to be replaced by a modern laundry.

The plant is now just a memory for those of us old enough to have experienced the lovely smell of freshly laundered clothes wafting through its big open doors. Like the Brickyard, Railway Station and Gas Works, the Youghal Steam Laundry is part of our earlier lives and as such will be treasured in our history.

CROSSING THE BLACKWATER AT YOUGHAL

Can you imagine a river so long that it rises in the mountains of North-east Kerry and enters the sea at Youghal? 'Broadwater' was the original name many centuries ago before it became *An Abha Mór* (the Big River) and later, Blackwater. As those names suggest, it is big and broad. Add strong and deep to give an idea of the great challenge it always presented to travellers.

Ardsallagh rises high over the eastern side and here an earthen Dún or Fort stood in early centuries to protect the native Irish fishermen and hunters. Later, the Danes ventured up-river in the 9th century to plunder Molanna Abbey at Dai Inis and Lismore, many times. On the more wooded western side of the river, the sizeable ivy-clad relics of Knights Templar of Rhincrew can still be seen on the hill top. The pilgrim knights built this fine fortress in the late 12th century to give them a commanding view of the river and estuary, plus a panorama from Ardmore to Youghal Bay.

As late as two centuries ago, there was still no bridge crossing this part of the river. It was crossed using a rope drawn, barge-like craft, from Tinnabinna on the Waterford side to the sloblands on

Timber Bridge across the Blackwater 1833 to 1883

the Cork side. To give an insight into how poor times were, people were carried over in this craft without charge but an animal was one penny for a return journey. When the Clashmore men would arrive at the loading stage, they would tie their animal to a nearby tree before crossing free in the barge. This was because they hadn't the penny to pay the animal's passage.

Landing on the mud-flats at the Cork side, they would then walk the mile to Youghal to do their shopping and bring out the bags of meal on their backs to the ferry. Crossing over again free to Tinnabinna, they would load up their donkey or pony before heading over Ardsallagh Hill for home. Such very laborious work - and all because they hadn't the penny to spare.

In 1833, a timber bridge was built to link up with a man-made causeway projecting to meet it from the Cork side. This bridge lasted until 1883 and so served for fifty years.

Next came the famous Youghal metal bridge and during the years of 1881, '82 and '83, while it was being constructed, a large number of local labourers found employment on the project. The conditions were very harsh for all workers, generally speaking, towards the end of that century. Times have since changed so much that it is hard for us, over a hundred years later, to imagine

'Kathleen and May' passing through the metal bridge 1883 to 1963

life without good working conditions. National health payments and widows' and orphans' pensions were unheard of. Couple that with poor safety measures, bad clothing, inadequate diet and rampant T.B. Such was the lot of the locals working on that metal bridge.

One story, which emphasises the above, tells that any worker found to be wearing a waistcoat during working hours was promptly sent home. Even in the middle of winter, it was felt that if a man could not work hard enough to keep himself warm in his shirt, he was not worth employing.

As the structure neared completion, it became clear that it would not be of uniform size. It was a most unusual bridge in that the Waterford half, with its thicker legs and higher railings, was far stronger than the Cork half. Apparently the two county authorities could not agree on a common plan and so each built its own half, regardless of the other's idea.

For eighty years that metal bridge carried the considerable Cork-Waterford traffic, although for its last few years, it was somewhat restricted by age.

Barrels of sand were placed along its length, through which the cars had to weave, to slow them up. Vibration was its biggest enemy as the rust ate deeper into its supports.

Because of those barrels on the bridge, the C.I.E. public buses could no longer cross over. They would park on their respective sides in special bay areas while the passengers walked across the bridge to the other bus. At 10.30 a.m., 3.30 p.m. and 7.30 p.m., every day, the buses would arrive simultaneously and, regardless of weather, the passengers would have to alight. A local hackney man, **Mick Ahern**, was hired by C.I.E. to bring the luggage and elderly passengers across in his car and trailer. Everybody else would brave the wind, rain and cold on that bleak connection. The Cork side especially was very exposed with its mere three-foot high railings, and pedestrians would crouch below them for imaginary protection. At least the Waterford part had six-foot high metal cross-sections to dispel any fears of being blown over the side.

A local character called Mick Keogh was a bus conductor in those years and was quick to see entertainment in any situation.

Bertie Doyle was his driver and they always worked together. Approaching the bridge on stormy days, Mick would walk back the aisle of the bus warning the passengers to keep low on the impending test of nerve.

"The last person blown over was never found," said Mick, as he wound up their fears. "And don't run back to me. I won't let you back on my bus," he would tease. Then, if some misfortunate had a bike with him on the bus, he would encourage him or her to ride it across the windswept river. Mick was merely being himself, a great funster, although strangers did not always see him like that.

One stormy day, a female traveller refused point-blank to cross the bridge. She would neither walk nor go in the taxi, such was her fear of water. Mick tried all kinds of bluff and persuasion to no avail. He even bluntly told her that she was not retracing her journey with him. The bus at the far side was still waiting. The woman had both vehicles delayed. Mick was at his wits end, but he was a crafty character with one last trick up his sleeve. Over the bridge came **Jack Rapley** in his small grey van with his wife **Chrissie** sitting beside him, and Mick waved him down.

"Would you ever bring this woman back into Youghal, out of my sight, because she's afraid to cross the water,' said Mick, as he winked at Jack. "Message received, you'll have to go into the back of the van, Mam," said Jack. Into the van she got and sat quietly down in the twilight. The vehicle did a fast U-turn before driving across the bridge quickly. When Jack opened the back door of the van over in the other county, the woman left out a mighty roar before she boarded the Waterford bus to continue her journey.

"Good thinking, Mick!"

A gate was erected at both ends to get traffic to stop before crossing and also to enforce the new five-ton weight limit. The gates were manned twenty-four hours a day and small timber houses were provided for the guardians. Sometimes at night, a driver would have to blow the horn to wake the man in the box who would sleepily appear to open the gate. Two giant drive-on weighing scales were used to check any vehicle likely to be over the five-ton limit.

Grain lorries would tow an empty trailer as far as the buttress approach road before transferring half of the lorry cargo to it. On reaching the other side, the whole load would be put back on the lorry again. The circus also had great trouble as they were only allowed to tow one wagon at the time across. Circus lorries could be towing three wagons from town to town and had to spend much time crossing over and back before hitching up the lot together to move off again.

In January 1963, the new concrete bridge was opened by Mr. Neil Blaney, T.D., linking the historical hills, half a mile up river, from the old site. It is far higher over the water than its predecessor and has no opening span, as tall masted ships no longer go up river. Happily no life was lost in the building of the new bridge, but sadly a man was drowned in the dismantling of the old one.

So the next time that you cross the Blackwater at Youghal, pause awhile. Notice the shags drying their wings as they stand like statues, the herons spaced on the water's edge silently fishing, and the oyster catchers so busy amongst the seaweed. Admire the lovely woodland hills rising high over the stream-lined bridge and imagine all the history this place has seen.

WHO CAN DO THE DOGGY PADDLE?

Nobody was allowed to swim in the Blackwater from the sluice at the slob-bank unless they had mastered the doggy paddle. It was the first stroke that the self-taught swimmers managed.

On the inland side of the river bank, was a small pool which was about two feet deep, and this was where we kept our hands on the bottom for our first imaginary swim. After many hours of splashing and frolicking, kicking the water behind us, came a slight sense of floating. Bit by bit, for longer and longer, the hands would be taken off the mud and a feeble attempt made at propulsion. This was called the doggy paddle - the hands making an up and down motion in near the chest, afraid to stretch them out fully for fear of going under.

I could never understand how my mother refused to accept that a swim in that small pool did not substitute for a bath. No matter how many swims we would have on a Saturday, she still had us in the bath that night. I remember arguing with her one day about it and the explanation I got was that there were no soap-suds in the small pool Now I understood! The following Saturday, I took the soap from the bathroom with me when gong for the swim. Such a laugh the pals had, as I tried to make a lather with cold fresh water and the bar of soap. But they had a bigger laugh when I lost the bar of soap in the water and had to go home without it. I went very willingly and quietly into the bath that night.

Having mastered the doggy paddle, it was time to go over the bank to the river, where the real swimmers were. That old sluice was like a quay with its great big cut stones coming straight up from the water which could be up to twenty feet deep at high tide. To small boys it was a huge challenge, a kind of coming-of-age in swimming.

Living at the north side of Youghal meant a walk of about two miles to the Strand and this exercise was kept for Sundays. Packed trains from Cork, bringing many characters to the seaside made the promenade the place to be then. But on week-days the slob bank was where the fun was. To dive from the top into the clear fresh water was heaven for the better swimmers while the newcomers (graduates from the small pool) coyly swam over and back across the width of the opening. The oldest swimmer was Mr. Sheridan, a nice old man from Tallow Street, who was over eighty. He would slowly amble out the bank with his great white beard, which reached to his trouser belt, blowing in the breeze. On entering the water, he belied his age and swam like a fish.

The way times have changed! No young fellow had a towel. To run out the grass-topped bank for a few hundred yards and back, was our drier. The original blow-drier! The odd time that an old comrade, home on holidays would arrive with a towel, it would be savoured by all. Such luxury ! Towel, how are you, what about the lads who had no togs? They would openly ask for the use of somebody else 's after the swim. It would be rinsed well in the water, squeezed, of course, then put on wet. That second phase lot would be out-of-pain in seconds - better to be in the water fully, than dry with a wet togs on. The out-of-pain was a very apt expression. It could be painful getting into deep water and the more one hesitated, the more the pain. Crawling down the seaweed-covered bank beside the sluice was the slow way to start and a person had to be careful not to slip. Those who did were in rather sorely. Brave and bold was the guy who started by diving or jumping from the top position - the shock could be terrible, followed by a few instinctive fast strokes back to the bank.

It was a male-only swimming area and I can never remember a female in the water at the sluice. They weren't discouraged, they just never came. Needless to mention, it occurred occasionally that, some lads who had no togs did not bother to wait for the second session and just dived in as naked as when they were born. This back-fired on a teenager when a man and wife came walking their dogs out along the bank, while he was still in the water. They knew him well and had a good long chat while he treaded water hoping that it wasn't too clear. As they left, the man's wife remarked on how long the swimmer was staying in the water and how much he must love it. Little did she know! Another incident like that was solved when the chap, who was perished in the water, pulled several handfuls of seaweed and draped it around his buttocks as he emerged. As everyone knows, seaweed is very slippery and by the time he reached his clothes, his cover was minimal.

No doubt, some of the best swimmers of the Youghal area served their apprenticeship at the sluice of the slob bank. Many of those later joined the British and Irish navies and when it came to the swimming and diving tests, the lads from the sluice were tops. Others went on to become Merchant Seamen. Tom Bennet, R.I.P., of Flemings Court was one of those, not forgetting the people who stayed at home to swim across the estuary of the Blackwater and back again on a summer's evening. No mean achievement was that, considering the tremendous force of the current.

Just now the slob bank is being widened to become an attractive tourist amenity as a riverside walk. On the western side, you have the low lands with their streams and pools sheltering many sea-bird and otters, while to the east the broad river rushes between West Waterford and East Cork to Youghal Bay.

How many emigrants in far off cities, while doing a few lengths of a nice warm pool think back to their first doggy paddle at the slob bank. A place of so many happy memories.

IN TOWN FOR ONE DAY ONLY

Back in the early 1950s, we small boys were hard to get out of bed at eight thirty in the morning to be at the Christian Brothers' school for nine. Our mother would call us many times before we would appear downstairs, still half asleep. There was one exception to this behaviour and that was on the morning that the circus came to town. To my mother's amazement, the alarm clock would be set by us and we would be up, dressed and out of the house by seven a.m. No doubt my father was the instigator of all this as he loved to talk about his own young days and circuses such as Lintons, Powells and Clarkes, Lyods, Lynie Farrells and Corvenios.

Down at Paddy Maher's paddock, we would climb on to the galvanised roof of the pig shed. This gave us a commanding view of the approach road and its ribbon of hawthorns was watched keenly for the first flash of a circus wagon's roof. Bread vans and post vans would mean a few false alarms, while all the time the talk was of circus.

An old man told us of his days as animal minder with Hannifords Circus. In those days there was no vehicle capable of transporting an elephant and so part of his job was to walk the animal from town to town. He would head off out the road after the night show and reach the new town sometime the next morning. We children would say, "Jack, what a lovely job to have!"

"Stop," he would answer. "If that elephant decided to lie down for a sleep out in the middle of nowhere, on a wet night, then all I could do would be to lie down beside him."

Another story about elephants comes to mind when a local character got a request from Mr. Fossett to bring the three circus elephants down to the local water trough. Off he went, walking down the middle of the main street with the three animals in tow. It was too much for some of the local boys on their way to school, and one said, "Dinny, give us an elephant!"

"Sorry, pal," said Dinny, "they're counted."

Suddenly the colours appear between the trees - there are many wagons like a large coloured snake making its way towards the town. Our spirits soar to new heights and the dancing on Paddy's galvanised roof wakes the whole neighbourhood.

The first circus lorry to enter the field is towing two trailers containing the canvas and poles. This is it. The big top has arrived! The tent men pace out an area before the sledge hammers commence their finely-timed ringing to drive the stakes into the hard ground. Following the stitching together of the quarters of canvas, we all crawl under it, in as far as the king-poles, and we help to pull up the tent.

Lucky was the boy who got a call from a wagon to go for a bucket of fresh water, as this usually meant a free pass to the matinee. Boys who had no pass and no money would wait for the performance to start before sneaking under the canvas sidewalls and promptly sitting up on the nearest seat. I remember one poor boy doing this only to find himself in the dearest seating area with well-dressed people sitting around him - and he with his elbows out through his jumper. One of the ring men noticed his shabby appearance and was about to quiz him when the boy cleverly turned to the man beside him to ask the time. Thinking that the well-dressed man had brought this poor child to the circus, the tent man moved away.

Before the end of the night show, props and excess chairs were moved out of the tent and packed away in trailers. Later, while the audience poured out under searchlights with the generators roaring nearby, the high seating was already being dismantled. Everyone with the circus was working on the pull-down. The acrobats, trapeze artists and clowns were all anxious that everything be packed away as quickly as possible in readiness for the early morning journey to the next town. After half an hour, the canvas was back down on the ground, with just the king-poles standing naked against the sky in a last salute to this town for another year.

SEASONAL GAMES OF CHILDHOOD

There is so much education today it makes one wonder where we got sufficient preparation for life. But think back to the seasonal games of childhood and there lies part of the answer, when imagination, improvisation and creativity at play were lessons that we never forgot.

Conkers

This was a game played by putting a hole in a chesnut, with a lace through it and holding it up to be hit by another. Two players took every second turn, until one of the chesnuts broke. The survivor became conker one and the game went on with another new chesnut challenger. Now and then an established conker 20 would meet up with a conker 30 and the winner would become 50. This was a boy's game and many the lad upped his conker in leaps and bounds by little white lies. No way of knowing, of course. Just believing made it all real.

"Don't hit me on the knuckles again, so shorten that string," youth would say. Or, "Keep that chesnut off the ground, the baby has one in his mouth!" a busy mother would shout.

Walking excursions took place out the country to the biggest chesnut tree to start the shelling of the tree with sticks and stones. There was great excitement when a large mature chesnut would peep forth from the spiky shell. "Put some up the chimney for next year. Smoked chesnuts are very hard to break." We never found out. Anything up the chimney, except Santa, was quickly forgotten.

Fag Cards:

Colourful cards of dogs or maybe trains were given free in packets of cigarettes and so were called 'fag-cards.' Competitions were played by flicking a card through the air and the winner was the one whose card went farthest. The cards could also be dropped on to the ground from chest height and the winner was the first to land a card on top of another. We were all anxious to befriend the smokers, that they might give us their fag cards. Gold Flake, Sweet Afton and Wild Woodbine are the brands of that time that come to mind.

Marbles:

The first marbles were made of clay and were easily crushed when trodden on. Some sour-faced adults would walk on our clay marbles deliberately to discourage us from taking over the footpath. Later came the glass ones and we always called them 'alleys.' Down on our knees we were, in short pants, on the smooth flagstones of the pavement, taking aim, shooting an alley at the top line. Abuse would comefrom the women with their baskets as they had to take a few steps on to the muddy roadway to get past the play. Shooting from straight in front of the 'lay' or shooting diagonally from the corner. Sharp-knuckle or rounded knuckles on the ground, to give every chance of winning those glassialleys.

Poor boys who had no marbles would offer to shoot for the bad player, hoping to win a few for themselves, enabling them to start up again.

Hoops:

Such fun as could be had with a plain bicycle wheel rim and a piece of stick to propel it with, off down the street at full belt, beating the hoop as it gathered speed. A gentle touch of the stick steered the hoop so accurately through the carts. Great exercise, no cost, a little bit noisy!

Cork Hill is very steep as one boy found out when, without thinking, he raced his hoop straight down the hill. After twenty yards it gathered speed and ran away from him, completely out of control. It headed for the right-angle at which the Hill meets North Main Street and he could only watch in panic. Across the bottom, facing up, was Fleming's Bakery Shop. Lovely big windows with small strips of wall-like pillars in between, seemed to stare innocently up the hill. The hoop was really moving as it bounded towards certain contact with the bakery.

The boy stopped to breathlessly wrap himself around a gas lamp and he peeped after the hoop as his ears awaited the sound of the crash. Then a loud bang was heard all over the area. But alas! it was steel on concrete as the contorted hoop went high into the air from a pillar between the windows. He hugged and kissed the gas-lamp. Life was good again.

As he headed for home, he walked over the buckled hoop. "I wonder who left that there?" said he, slyly to himself.

Pickey:

A piece of broken statue was, most often, the chalk used to mark out the 'beds' for the game of pickey on the pavement. Only never let anyone's mother recognise the piece of 'chalk' or we'd get the holy water splashed all over us. Many were the variations of this game with the piece of wood. Plain pickey or hopskotch were the main two played. Girls were the masters here, and it was considered sissy-ish for boys to be caught playing it. A bit like what was thought of skipping games - the girls' area! The singing as they turned the rope was delightful. Songs and rhymes passed down through generations and were remarkable for their local accents.

Tops:

Spinning tops were hard to get going before being whipped down the street with what was a simple twig and a piece of string. Road surfaces were not good and so the spinning tops were few. There were two kinds - one was an A line heavy type which was hard to start. The other T-shape top was lighter and a little easier to manage. Many the window was broken by a flying top as the over-zealous lad used all his strength in a last effort to keep it going. Any boy responsible for the breaking of glass was never known to ask for his top back. He just ran! God be with the days.

Comics:

Kit Carson and Buck Jones were the small 64-page comics in a kind of pocket book size. You also had the Classics Illustrated which were very colourful and told stories like Huckleberry Finn, Robinson Crusoe and Gulliver's Travels. The comics were linked via our creative minds to what we saw in the cinema, so that the picture strips came alive for us. Before the coming of T.V. , a weekly visit to the local Picture Hall for a fourpenny matinee was the highlight of the week. Afterwards imagination was given free reign as we galloped up the main street on the way home, pretending to be Roy Rogers or Hopalong Cassidy. Easy to understand then how the comics had us on the trail again, riding imaginary horses.

Swopping was commonplace in every street, just after tea-time, to share the thrills on the colour pages. One boy I remember would go house to house with a big bunch of comics looking for swops. This lad was different in his dealings in that he insisted always in trading for better material. Two comics without covers would be offered for a new one. Or a slightly torn one for a perfect specimen. He knew that we were gasping for a read and that what we had, we would already have read over and over. Apparently, his collection of comics was truly exceptional and he treasured them. One cannot help but wonder what happened to that collection and how they would be valued nowadays.

Taylors Lane
L to R: Paddy O'Sullivan, Tommy Ryan, Pat O'Reilly, Michael Lee
and Derry Power

THE LEAGUE OF THE CROSS

The League of the Cross, an abstention from drink society, was first housed at 124 North Main Street before twin four-floor buildings were acquired at Catherine Street to make *The League* as we now know it. Originally, one of the two was the house of a Customs Officer and so was in close proximity to the busy quays of the last century. A doorway was made into a window just north of the present front door and a stairway was removed to make the buildings into one large unit. As well, the big hall on the south side was purchased and this was invaluable for gymnastics and film shows.

Every now and then, there comes an individual who has the will, ability, energy and time to motivate others and mould them into a collective unit for the benefit of all. **Fr.Michael Aherne** was just such a person. He was a dynamo to those around him and being part of the League of the Cross was the challenge he needed. As well as all the sports facilities like gymnastics, boxing and billiards, the League had a reading room, band room and concert hall. In those early years, trades like brass work, copper-beating and carpentry were taught. Because education was not compulsory, with children leaving school as young as ten years old, a night school was established to teach the three Rs - reading, 'riting and 'rithmatic.

A local man remembers that as a boy in the League, he saw a few young men get up to devilment. In the course of their brass-work class, they brazed two ha'pennies together to get a two-headed coin for pitch and toss games. A few bob was won before the coin was noticed.

A blacksmith, **Garrett Revins**, had a forge and yard at Friar Street, near the spot where the Regal Cinema now stands. He was a staunch member of the League and tried hard to abide by the abstention from drink rule. Any member unable to abstain went down the following Monday night to take the pledge all over again with Fr. Aherne.

Garrett's problem was that the farmers often insisted on bringing him next door to Dickenson's pub to have a drink, before paying him for shoeing their horses. If he didn't oblige, he wouldn't get paid. He told the story himself of emerging from Dickenson's with a farmer one night and they almost bumped into Fr. Aherne. The priest was quick to remark, "I'll see you on Monday night, Garrett."

Around the 1920s, in the reading room, you could find people like **Paddy Dunne, Alf Tudgie** and **Con Hickey,** all from Cork Hill; **Tom Sullivan** of Windmill Lane, **Tom White** and **Dick Morgan** of North Main Street, and **Patsy Aherne** from a few doors away at Catherine Street.

An old friend tells of playing alleys (marbles) as a child with his pals on the pavement flags at Catherine Street. He knocked out (won) several alleys with one shot and he stretched forward quickly to grab them. Just then, Fr. Aherne, who had been trying to pass, fell over him. The priest gave the lad a slap on the ear and off he ran, crying to his mother. When he told her his story, she asked him which ear and when he pointed to it, she gave him a slap on the other one. "Be more careful, young fella," she shouted at him. The next time that the lad encountered Fr. Aherne, the priest gave him a penny - which was a lot in those days - by way of an apology.

Ernest Bush came to Youghal with the Border Regiment and loved the place so much that he stayed on to marry **Ellen Sawse** of North Main Street. He was a great cornet player and was for many years leader of the brass band of the League of the Cross. My own memory of him is playing the last post outside the British Legion Club on Remembrance Day. Even though old in years by then, he was a marvellous player.

On the day of the Annual Eucharistic Procession in town, the League of the Cross would put on a fine show. A big long banner on two poles would be carried up front. Then the brass band would march ahead of the large membership. All the men wore a special green sash and the boys wore a smaller one. The building would be almost hidden with flowers and greenery for the occasion and the roadway would be criss-crossed high up with rows of bunting.

In the 1960s, limited improvements were done on the ground floor and for awhile the billiards, boxing and reading rooms were in business again. A launderette was also installed for the older citizens to wash clothes. Senior members at this time in the reading room were Jack Forrest, Christy Kenefick and Ned Clancy. **Bob McGrath** must be mentioned and a lot will remember him as the caretaker who lived on the top floor. He seemed a bit stiff to us but, God knows, he had to be.

Over the years it was the meeting place for the G.A.A., Legion of Mary, Pioneers, Fr. Barry's choir, Irish dancers, A.A., Bingo, concerts, Senior Citizens Welfare Association and Meals-on-Wheels.

The building is now being renovated from the ground to the chimney pots. A team of young men, under the guidance of **Derry McCarthy**, are dong a great job. The over-all motivator is **Dean St. John Thornhill, P.P.**. Very soon, this historical hall will cater again for the needs of the people.

A25 Diesel train leaving Youghal.
Photo Colm Creedon, Railway Historian.